Dorothy Robbins Talanca
April 19, 2022

Miss Sutton Does Things Differently!
Copyright 2022 Dorothy Robbins Talavera
Delanco, New Jersey

ISBN: 978-1-66782-798-8

Front cover photos: Emma, Essie and baby Oscar Sutton, c. 1886; Essie's official student nurse photo taken at the Philadelphia Hospital Training School for Nurses, 1903; tram ticket from trip to Egypt, 1920; postcard sent from Constantinople; Essie's passport, 1918. Photos owned by Dorothy Robbins Talavera

Back cover photo: Essie (on donkey) and a friend at the pyramids and sphynx, 1920. Photo used with permission of owner.

Miss Sutton Does Things Differently!

A Young Woman's Odyssey from Farm to International Relief Worker

By Dorothy Robbins Talavera

This book is dedicated to the generations of strong, brave women in my family who paved the way for me, and to my daughters, granddaughters, nieces and cousins who carry the tradition on. Thank you.

Table of Contents

*Our thoughts and imaginations are the only real limits
to our possibilities.*

**— Dr. Arison Swett Marden, 1897
Copied into Essie's 1916 diary**

Preface

Alice Estella Sutton was a real person. She was born December 1, 1874 on a farm in Springfield Township, Burlington County, New Jersey. Her long life took her to what seemed to be the ends of the Earth, in occupations that were unlikely for a girl such as she. She lived to age 80, passing away in Saratoga, New York on August 15, 1955. By then, she had lived in some of the most exciting cities in the world and worked in places covering half the globe.

Aunt Essie, as everyone around here called her, was my grandfather's sister. She was known for her adventurous spirit, her intellect, her knowledge of the Bible, her outspokenness, her practical, unsentimental nature, and her quirkiness. She was a devoted letter-writer and diarist, producing volumes of daily entries. I have those diaries, along with dozens of letters she wrote to various members of the family, and her photograph album. Her comments are always factual, brief, and without emotion or judgement. The quotes that appear throughout the book are taken directly from her work. Her down-played facts have been confirmed and supplemented by articles from newspaper archives, Red Cross nursing records and issues of the Red Cross newsletter The Acorne, which Essie saved.

Both Essie and her older sister Emma defied the customs of the day. Well into what was then referred to as "spinsterhood" (not marrying), each made monumental changes to her life, moving far away from the farm their family had always known. Neither ever saw herself as brave, nor did they boast about their experiences. They were not famous. Yet, looking at them within the context of history, they were ordinary young women doing extraordinary things during times of great change and upheaval.

We do not know what prompted the sisters to make the decisions they did. Essie never reveals any of that in her diaries. How did they discover these opportunities? How did they raise the money needed to take advantage of them? What did their relatives think of them? Contemplation of these questions is left to the reader.

This book focuses on a period in Essie's life that finishes with her participation in one of the greatest refugee relief efforts in history. All of the events really happened to her. It is written in her voice, and I did not correct her grammar, spelling or punctuation. My intention in writing the book is to make sure this remarkable woman and her accomplishments are remembered.

Dorothy Robbins Talavera
Delanco, New Jersey
August 2021

PART I

"As is my custom to write what I do on the day, I go in the particulars."

That is the first entry in my diary on December 1, 1900 – my 26th birthday. I had always started each diary entry with a weather report; the weather is so important to farmers. *Saturday, February 21: Clear, cold; Sunday, March 1: snow all day; Saturday, May 18: fair, warm; Sunday, June 2: hot, clear;* and so on.

For more than half a century I had the habit of journaling almost every day. That's how I can remember so well what has happened to me in my long life. It has turned out a little different than anyone expected.

My name is Alice Estella Sutton. What a fancy, elegant name! Both my first and middle name come from books that were popular when I was born. Alice was a brave girl in Lewis Carroll's two recent books about Wonderland and the Looking Glass. Estella was a character who overcame all odds in Charles Dickens' book <u>Great Expectations</u>. But nobody called me either of those names – ever! My family called me Essie, a good, solid, practical name – like me. Soon, people on four continents would know me as Miss Sutton!

When I was born, the Civil War had been over for ten years. Every family knew a boy who had been killed, or who had simply disappeared. My Aunt

Beulah never got over her son Joseph's death from infection after he got his leg shot off at the Battle of Bull Run in Manassas, Virginia. Mother kept all the letters her cousin Joseph and her brother William had written to her during the war. The letters were tied up with a ribbon and kept in her dresser drawer. That's how we knew they were special to her. Lots of the men around here were crippled up from their injuries and harbored dark secrets. No one talked about the war with us children, but we knew there had been one. Our friend Mr. R. visited the school on the anniversary of the end of the war to tell the students about his experiences, and all we remember about that visit was a bearded old man muttering "shots and shells" over and over. We were embarrassed about hearing it. Later, I would learn first-hand what war was like, and I would come to have a dark side of my own.

Life on our farm in Burlington County, New Jersey was hard work. In addition to Mother and Father, we were nine children: my brother Walter, sister Emma and I were the eldest, with Clif, Mary Ella, Rob, Howard, John and Oscar following us like stairsteps. There always were little ones running around, needing to be looked after. Mother's father lived with us too. Everybody we knew lived pretty much like we did.

1881 - A Terrible Summer

The summer I was seven years-old was pretty awful. My grandfather died. He had asthma, which gave him problems breathing. He couldn't help with the farm work, like he wanted to. I remember the day he died. There was a lot of whispering behind closed doors, and people coming in and out of our house all day. It scared me. And then, there was The Balloon Incident.

My brothers Walter and Clif came running into the house, shouting about something that had landed in our field. Clutched in their grubby hands was a broken rubber balloon and a printed notice offering a new suit of clothes and a five-dollar reward to whoever found it. Mr. John Wanamaker was opening a big department store in Philadelphia, and sent out this balloon as a publicity stunt. It had sailed almost forty miles, all the way across the Delaware River to our farm! So far away!

Well, the boys started arguing over who saw the balloon first and would get the clothes and the five dollars. New clothes that were not hand-me-downs were an unheard-of luxury. Our family didn't have much money. Nobody did. There had been the Long Depression throughout the nation during my whole life. In fact, Father was getting ready to take a job out West for a while to pay off some of our debts. New clothes from an expensive store in the city! And, for free! And a large cash reward too! This was such good luck! Imagine!

Father and the boys walked the six miles to the station in Burlington, and took the train and the ferry into Philadelphia to claim the prize.

Pretty soon, neighbors got word about the excitement, and our good luck turned into disaster. The big newspaper in Philadelphia printed a terrible article about us, without even asking us any questions! Everyone in our community was talking about it. The paper said that we had a dreadful family fight over the prize, and how Grandfather died because of it. They said Father stole all our valuables and abandoned us. They said we owed more money on the farm than anyone could ever pay off. Mother felt like she couldn't hold her head up in church anymore because of the gossip.

Mother was angry. None of what people were saying was true, so she did something very brave. She wrote something called an "affidavit" telling the real facts, and got important people to sign it and swear it was the truth. She wrote that Grandfather had been sick. She told how she and Father had talked about him going West for a long time, because he once had a good-paying job there. Then, she mailed that affidavit to the newspaper. Two weeks later, the paper printed a short paragraph near the last page quoting what Mother wrote. They never did apologize for all the hurt their story caused. I cut that little clipping out of the paper and kept it for the rest of my life. I wanted Mother's version to be the one I remembered.

It was hard with Father away. At that point, there were eight of us children. Oscar wasn't born yet. Little Johnny was an infant, and Howard was just learning to walk. It was up to us older children to do farm and household chores. Eighty acres is a lot to take care of! Both Mother and Father had lots of brothers and sisters. Most of them were farmers and lived close by. Some of our uncles and friends helped by operating the farm machinery, but my brothers, sisters and I tossed the hay onto the hay wagon and picked the fruits and vegetables. My sister Emma and I washed all the laundry in a big kettle of boiling water over an open fire.

The next summer was even worse. My sister Mary Ella died. She was only six years old. We buried her little casket in the beautiful, peaceful country cemetery called Cedar Hill, where she could be with generations of our family members who have gone before. She will never be alone.

1900 – A New Century

The twentieth century! My! How exciting! Little could I imagine the changes that would take place in the coming years. Father had returned home from out west with the money we needed to save the farm. Soon after that, baby Oscar arrived. By now, he was already a teenager.

Our family had spread out. Walter went to sea. Emma was teaching, and boarding with a family near her school. She often came home for the weekend. Howard, and John lived with Mother and Father on our farm. Oscar was living on the Hancock farm as a hired hand. He was only fifteen, but he was a hard worker.

My brothers Clif and Rob bought their own farm a few miles away from the old home place, and I lived with them to keep house. It was a lot of work taking care of those two men and keeping up with all the chores of daily life.

Every day was so busy. There was something to do every minute of the day.

> *"Sat. June 15, 1900: The boys made two screen doors for the kitchen, as it was raining, they could do nothing else."*

We raised all our own food, and there was lots of work involved in preserving it so we could eat for the year. Sometimes there was extra for us to sell at the open-air market where other local farmers sold their fruits, vegetables, eggs, and live animals. Freezers and refrigerators had not been invented yet, so we had to preserve all the food we would eat for the rest of the year. There were no grocery stores, nor was there any out-of-season produce shipped in from other parts of the world. All summer long I was busy preserving fruit and vegetables for the winter. I was proud of the number of jars I could put up. Putting up food (also known as "canning", even though we used glass jars instead of metal cans) was hard, sweaty work. It always took place during the hottest days of summer, when the produce was ripe. The stove blazed away all day. We had to sterilize the empty glass jars and zinc lids with steam, wash, peel and cut up the produce, cook the fruit in syrup and the vegetables in brine, fill the jars with the hot contents, cap the jars and process them in vats of boiling water. We had special tongs for lifting the hot jars out of the water bath to cool. There were crocks full of fermenting sauerkraut and pickles. The whole house smelled like whatever we were canning. It was a comforting aroma – assurance that we would be well fed all winter. Our cellar shelves were lined with colorful jars.

"Sat. June 15: I canned 15 jars of strawberries today."

"Sat. Jun 29: Emma helped me pick over the gooseberries, and I put them in the jars tonight. We had our last strawberries for supper."

"Wed. July 10: I put up 10 jars of pie cherries"

"Fri. Sept 13: I canned sixteen jars of tomatoes today."

"Tues. Sept 17: Emma came up this afternoon and brought nearly two baskets of peaches. She helped me put them in the jars. She did not go home until after supper. I did my ironing this evening."

"Sat. Oct. 3: I put up five jars of pears today beside doing the other work."

We also butchered and processed our own hogs and chickens. We salted or smoked and dried meat to preserve it. I melted the lard and saved it for baking, and made sausage and scrapple. Nothing goes to waste. I learned later in life the people in other parts of the United States don't know about scrapple, made from the tiniest scraps of the animal. What a shame. It is delicious.

Our relatives often came to help out with the work, and usually stayed for supper. Those big family dinners were so lively and full of interesting conversation! Here is what I wrote in my diary about what was just a typical day:

> "*Sat. Jan. 1, 1900: We rose about six o'clock this morning and had breakfast at seven; Clif, Rob and I were all that were here. Oscar went home yesterday afternoon to go to Philadelphia with Emma, he came back here this evening. I made bread and that was all the Saturday work I did. We killed hogs yesterday, one weighing 400 lb., the other 132. Uncle Jud killed two here also; all of his family were here to dinner but cousins Bertha and Bessie. Mother, John and Father were here to help us. The boys cut the hogs up this morning and I got the lard all rendered by night. I got through my work by 8:30 o'clock and took my bath after the rest had gone to bed; and I went at about 11 o'clock.*"

Uncle Jud and Aunt Annie had the farm that bordered ours. They often helped us with farm work and stayed to supper. Aunt Annie and Mother were sisters. We saw them a lot. We would just walk across the field to see each other. Other cousins lived close enough for frequent visits on foot, horseback or in farm wagons. Growing up on a farm, there was room for healthy children to rough-house, play and run when the chores were finished.

My brothers were very strong and athletic. Baseball was a great sport to play when there were lots of brothers and cousins around, and our boys loved it. They were good players, especially Rob. Oscar even played on the high school team. Several of the neighboring towns had their own teams, which played each other. My diary is full of entries about the places where they went to play: Beverly, Rancocas, Columbus, White Hill, and others.

> "*Sat. May 28, 1904: Four of our boys and five of the Jacksonville boys making a baseball team played against the Burlington High School team, on which Oscar plays. Jacksonville was defeated, the score was 8 to 10. Uncle Wes went in to see the game.*"

Our large family had lived in this area for so many generations that we were related by marriage to almost everybody. Lots of people stopped by, so we kept up on the news. We knew who had a baby, who was sick, and who died. One girl cousin had a copy of Peterson's Magazine, full of the most wonderful pictures and descriptions of the latest Paris fashions. We poured over it together as children, dreaming of a day when we would wear such creations. It didn't matter that in our small farming community we would never have an occasion to display this type of finery. Although I never considered myself to be pretty, I loved nice clothes.

Back then, almost everyone went to church. I could mark the passing of each week by going to Friday evening prayer meetings, Sunday school and church on Sunday morning, and Sunday night Christian Endeavour. There, we met and socialized with many friends and relations. I also taught the children's Sunday school class. Even though Clif, Rob and I had moved to our own farm, we continued to attend the little church in Jacksonville where our family had always gone. It now was about a 5-mile walk each way to get there. Sometimes we would get a ride home in a neighbor's wagon. Rob usually went with me, but Clif didn't go.

Despite family visits and play, there was a regular schedule for chores. Looking back in my diaries I see that my days were spent cooking, cleaning, washing, and sewing. Every Monday was wash day. Farmers' clothes get really dirty. There were no electric washing machines, dryers or irons. There was no laundry detergent. I would boil a big kettle of water on our coal stove, and soak the clothes and other items in it. Then, I would scrub them on a washboard with the lye soap I had made from ashes and the fat of the animals we had butchered. Finally, I hung the heavy wet clothes on the line to dry. In the winter time, the wet clothes would freeze stiff right there on the clothesline! All of our clean laundry needed ironing. The pile of shirts, dresses, pants, underwear, sheets, table clothes, and napkins seemed endless! They were all made of wool, cotton, silk, or linen. There was no polyester or drip-dry clothing then. I would set the heavy metal iron on top of the stove to heat it up, dampen the clothes slightly, then quickly pass the iron over the damp clothes to press out all the wrinkles. A cloud of steam whooshed up around my head as soon as the hot iron touched the damp fabric. I had to keep the iron moving so I wouldn't scorch or burn the fabric. There is nothing like the smell of clean, freshly pressed laundry!

I made all of my own clothes, as well as most things for my sister and brothers. By making clothing repairs for other people, I had saved enough money from my sewing to attend the famous McDowell Dressmaking School when it began offering classes in Philadelphia. I went into the city on the train every Wednesday morning for a class that began at 11:00. What an experience! The newspaper advertisement for it had caught my attention: "*We Lead Them All!! The McDowell Dressmaking School is the largest and best in the country. It is the only school in the city that has the reputation of giving their pupils just what they advertise. We teach everything from foundation to finish, how to draft every style garment by the McDowell system, which is acknowledged to be the simplest, easiest and most accurate system in existence.*" There I learned how to make patterns and construct those elaborate Paris designs I had longed for with my cousin. What a world of glamour I observed! I am proud of my certificate of completion of the course.

Once it became known that I had learned so much, more women began paying me to make dresses, chemises and undergarments for them. My diaries show that every moment not spent cooking, canning or cleaning was spent at the treadle sewing machine or doing hand finishing work. My eyes got tired. They have always been weak, and I wore thick spectacles.

"*Fri. Apr. 26: I finished my dark calico dress, that I started last winter, last week.*"

"*Sat. Apr. 27: I started to make my old light dress over.*"

"*Wed. May 1: I worked on my light dress today but I think I shall put it away and finish it next summer.*"

"*Wed. July 31: Emma spent the day with us. I got her underwaist done, also trimmed her hat. I cut out a gingham dress for her and I.*"

Even though our growing and preserving season was a summertime activity, there was still lots of hard work in the winter. There were many mill ponds around here. Mill ponds were reservoirs of water diverted from creeks, used to power water wheels. These wheels ran the giant mill stones that ground grain into flour or rotated the huge belts that ran factory machinery. There were no electric machines then.

Long, cold winters produced thick ice on any body of water. Some of our neighbors had ice houses – low structures that were mostly below ground level where huge blocks of ice would be stored for warm weather refrigeration. When the streams and ponds were thick with ice, the men would cut blocks of ice from them with big saws, then drag the blocks to shore hitched to teams of horses. The blocks were taken to the ice house, covered with sawdust and straw, where the ice would last almost all summer. None of the farms in our family had an ice house.

> "Tues. Dec. 18, 1900: Rob went to help G. Haines thrash today. Clif took the team and help T.B. Allison fill his ice house. Rob and I walked up to the Village to night to go over the exercise for the Christmas entertainment to be held Friday evening."

> "Wed. Dec. 19, 1900: Rob took the team and helped T. B. Allinson fill his ice house. Clif went to help G. Haines thrash today. Rob and Oscar went skating this evening."

> "Mon. Jan. 7, 1901: I washed this morning. Clif went to help finish filling T.B. Allinson 's ice house this morning. The boys went to skate on the Mill Pond."

We all enjoyed ice skating, although I didn't do it as much as the boys. After the work was done, we would strap iron blades to our shoes, and head for the frozen-solid streams and ponds

> "Sat. Dec. 15, 1900: The boys went to Burlington for a load of manure. The boys went skating on the old creek this evening; the first this winter. Herbert Kimble brought a pair of boxing gloves over this evening and he, Howard, and Ollie Styer with our boys played with them for a little while."

"Thur. Feb. 27, 1901: The boys went skating on "The Old Creek" this afternoon."

"Sat. Feb. 29, 1901: Mother was not very well. but the boys went skating on the Mill Pond. I had to stay home."

Our dairy cows produced milk all year round. I churned butter and made cottage cheese from our fresh milk. The boys hand milked the cows, squirting the warm liquid into buckets. Then, they poured it into 3-foot-high steel milk cans which they hauled into Burlington where the milk was bottled for sale. When roads were clear, we loaded the heavy milk cans into our horse-drawn farm wagon.

None of our country roads were paved; they were all dirt roads. When it rained, they were muddy and difficult to travel on. It was better when there was ice or packed snow on the ground to provide a solid surface. We had a sleigh for us to use on those days. There was so much snow back then! We had to clear our own way through the snow and ice; there were no snowplows sent out by the town or county government. There were accidents and injuries that we had to tend to ourselves.

"Mon Jan 12: High winds, getting colder, I washed and dried the clothes in the house."

"Sat. Feb 21: Clear, cold; John and I took a sleigh ride to Uncle Jud's this a.m. I ought to have stayed home."

"Sun Mar 1: Snow all day. H. winds p.m. & evening; Four telegraph poles & our phone wire were broken in front of the house. Emma could not go to the city for the storm."

"Mon Mar 2, 1914: Snowing all day; not more than 20 poles standing between here & Burl. Howard & John took the milk to Burlington, Walter went with them, gone over 5 hours, had to dig snow & cut telegraph wires, a wire flew & hit Howard, punctured eyeball, looks bad."

No one had telephones then. We knew that Mr. Alexander Graham Bell had invented something that would carry a human voice over a wire, but we couldn't imagine that it would be more than just a novel toy. The telegraph was what was used to send information quickly over long distances. Our family had no use for it because we always wrote letters to each other, but newspapers depended on the telegraph to get the facts about events of the day. We always read the newspaper to find out what was happening around us. Radios, televisions and the Internet had not yet been invented. In fact, we would have laughed at the very idea of such outlandish things!

I always loved the Christmas season. So much excited preparation! We always decorated the church.

"Thur. Dec. 20, 1900: Rob went to help trim the church today; I should have gone but I made a star and Rob and I covered letters with tinsel; so I did not have time."

"Fri. Dec. 21, 1900: It commenced snowing this afternoon at 1 o'clock and snowed hard until after dark. Rob and I drove down to the church to put the letters and stars up and two small trees. Rob and I walked up this evening; I wore my boots through the snow. The church was over half full of people but we did not have the entertainment. Clif and Rob went home to help kill a beef this morning."

"Sun. Dec. 23, 1900: Rob, Oscar and I walked up to S.S. and church this morning. Mother and Howard came up this afternoon, and brought us some Christmas presents. Emma, Howard and John gave us a pretty mantel clock that strikes the half hour as well as the hour. Mother gave Clif and Rob each a necktie, and gave me two glass sauce dishes, a gingham apron, a pair of stockings, a fancy plate to put on the mantel, and a china box for the bureau and a dozen napkins given by either Emma or Mother. They went home before supper for fear it would rain. Rob was the only one that went to the C.E. meeting from here."

"Mon. Dec. 24, 1900: Rob, Oscar and I walked up to the S.S. Christmas entertainment this evening; the church was full. I gave each one of my scholars a handkerchief. Fannie gave me a nice linen one. Miss Ella gave

Clif and Rob each two with initials. Katie Kimble gave me her picture. Oscar got a Bible for saying his catechism."

"Tues. Dec. 25, 1900: Christmas. I churned this morning; the first time since the second week in October. I had a little over 3 pounds of butter. We had dinner about four o'clock. In the evening Emma, Howard and John came up and all of Uncle Jud's family but Bessie; she had gone to spend the week with Cousin Blanche at Lumberton. We spent the evening playing games, had candy, popcorn balls, pears, and apples to eat. They all went home about 11 o'clock."

One day we got the dreadful news that the President of the United States, Mr. McKinley, had been assassinated by an anarchist during a visit to the Pan American Exposition in Buffalo, New York. What was this world coming to? All that talk made us curious. When Emma came home that weekend, she wondered how we could get to Buffalo ourselves to see the "Pan Am" and where Mr. McKinley was shot. Well, she figured out a way to do it. She worked out all our travel arrangements and who we would stay with. We had some relatives in that part of the state who recommended families renting rooms near the Exposition. The two of us left on the 6 o'clock a.m. train to Buffalo on a dark October morning. We had never been so far from home! It was a thrilling adventure, and I knew I wanted to travel again.

"Oct. 16, 1901: We went in the Temple of Music in the afternoon and saw the spot where the late President stood when he was shot. There was a crowd around the building nearly all the time waiting to get in. We waited there quite a while before getting in; we were afraid we would be unable to get in. We stayed for the illumination and the fire-works in the evening; they were the finest I ever saw. We enjoyed the Pan very much, saw many interesting things. Sunday morning we went to the church; we did not like it."

Life was full, but then Mother's health began giving her problems. She couldn't eat much, developed terrible sores on her legs and feet, and could hardly walk. She went to several different doctors, who all diagnosed different things. One thought it was blood poisoning, and treated her for that. Finally it was diagnosed as diabetes, something we didn't know much about in those days. She tried very hard to keep up with all the farm work, but Emma was doing all the chores for her. This was hard when Emma was teaching full time. She had been living near her school, but gave that up to move home and take care of Mother.

Mother's foot developed gangrene. The doctor and nurse came out to the farm from Burlington; we cleaned and prepared the north bedroom for surgery, and that afternoon Mother's foot was amputated. The nurse stayed with us for a week. Despite the surgery, Mother grew weaker and weaker. Three months later she died, surrounded by many of her loved ones. We buried her at Cedar Hill, next to her beloved little daughter Mary Ella.

> *"Mon May 18, 1903: Walter went to Burlington this morning to get Dr. Black's operating table and instruments, also the trained nurse (a Miss Nichols of Philadelphia) who will stay a week. She, with my help, fixed the north room for the operation; I had cleared it out before she came. The Doctor brought another nurse with him, to give the either. They got here about one o'clock. The operation was performed at two and took about two hours. Mother was conscious again at five o'clock in the afternoon. Doctor called again this evening."*

> *"Thurs. July 2, 1903: Mother is very weak; does not say anything except when I ask a question; sleeps nearly all the time, is slipping away."*

> *Fri July 3, 1903: Mother lost consciousness a little after 1 o'clock this morning; and passed away at fifteen minutes of seven this evening. Uncle Wes, Aunt Marty, Aunt Abbie, Aunt Annie, and all the family but Cliff and Rob were present."*

> *"Wed. July 8, 1903: The funeral was yesterday; the boys were pall bearers and nearly all of our relatives were here.*

Two of the things people still remember about Mother are her beautiful eyes, and her kindness. I remember her bravery and how hard she tried to be part of our farm life, even when she was so sick and could barely walk. I will always miss her.

****

Farmers don't make much money. We had plenty to eat, with all the crops and animals we raised, but never had much cash for expenses such as taxes. We sold our wheat and extra produce, but we were always living on a tight budget. I earned some from making dresses for friends, and the boys sometimes went to work part time in the mills, if farm work was slow. Little by little, the good pay and predictable schedule of factory work began to lure my brothers away from the farm. Walter was already at sea, Howard went to Buffalo looking for work, Oscar moved to Cleveland to go to technical school; then Rob moved into Burlington to work in the Devlin Steel Mill. Eventually, Clif moved to Detroit to work in an automobile factory. None of us had ever ridden in an automobile, but there were some around. People referred to an automobile as a "machine".

Clif and Rob gave up farming and sold theirs in November 1904 for $25 an acre. Uncle Jud bought all our horses and walked them across the field to his own barn. I moved back to the old home place, my father's farm where we had all grown up. It seemed very empty without Mother and my brothers and sister. It was just Father, John, and me. So many changes! Christmas was very different and somber this year.

> *"Sun Dec 25, 1904: Christmas. It snowed all day. Temperature 28 degrees. We got up about 7 o'clock. Rob went to church, then came home with us. It was so stormy, we had just plain meals. The boys went to bed at 9 o'clock. I am going to bed at 11. Rob and I wondered where we will be next year this time."*

1905 – My Turn to Leave Home

The notebooks in which I wrote my diaries were free advertising gifts from insurance companies. Inserted among the blank calendar pages were wonderful world maps and tables with important facts. Each month started with a list of risks the farmer faced that month and how to prevent them. I read them all. From these pages I learned that the distance from Philadelphia to San Francisco was 3,100 miles; the population of New Jersey in 1900 was 1,883,669; the postal rate for delivering a one- pound package to a local city was $0.05. There was a chart for calculating the amount of interest one would have to pay on any loan amount, which all farmers should know. The back of the diary had a place to record expenses, cash on hand and income, so I kept careful records all my life. It was the maps that kept drawing my attention.

Whenever I found an interesting paragraph in the newspaper, or some kind of inspirational saying, I would cut it out and save it in my diary. Looking at some of them now, I remember how those yellowed clippings got me through difficult times.

> *"To have what we want is riches; but to be able do without is power"* MacDonald

"It is better to be true than to be popular; better to be sincere that to be sought after; better to be kind than to be brilliantly witty and entertaining."

"Concise thinking is a splendid help to concise talking. Loose, flabby sentences, too weak and lacking in force to command attention, are the result of loose, flabby thinking. Have your idea definitely in mind, then force yourself to enunciate it."

With Mother gone, and Emma away teaching, my life continued to be full of cleaning, washing, cooking, and women's chores for the men at my father's farm. I was already thirty years old, a plain looking spinster. I knew from watching others what my fate would be if I stayed here. "Maiden ladies" such as I cared for their aging parents, then bounced around among their married siblings to become housekeepers and favorite aunts. Was it too late for me? Surely, there must be something more!

During that week the nurse from Burlington stayed with us following Mother's surgery, I spent many hours talking with her about her training and her work. It sounded exciting and perfect for me. I had saved all my sewing money, so I sent a letter of application to nursing school.

I don't know how Father felt about it; he didn't talk much since Mother died. One by one we were leaving him. It was not unusual for a young woman from around here to become a teacher. Emma was one, and so were others like Walter's girlfriend Sarah. The women taught until they got married, then gave it up. Emma wasn't married, but she came home on the train almost every weekend. No one from here had ever become a nurse.

In a letter dated April 15, 1905 I got wonderful news from The Pennsylvania Hospital Training School for Nurses in Philadelphia. It told me I was offered the position of Probationer, to begin in one month.

Oh my! There was so much to get ready in such a short time – sewing, shopping, seeing the dentist!! The acceptance letter told me I was to take with me *"four gingham dresses to be made with plain skirts and shirtwaists, the sleeves to be finished at the wrist with a band with two buttons; twelve large white aprons without bibs made of bleached muslin; a good supply of underclothing plainly made; one small and two large bags for soiled linen; two pairs of noiseless shoes with rubber heels; a wrapper; a watch with a secondhand; a plain napkin ring with the name of the owner."* It said I was to have my teeth tended to and get a doctor's certificate of recent successful vaccination.

> *"Mon. May 15, 1905: I left home this morning about 8 o'clock & reached here, Penna hospital, about 9:30 and went just as soon as I was shown to my room & had time to change my dress, which was 11 o'clock, on duty on B ward."*

How lucky was I to be at Pennsylvania Hospital! Miss Lucy Walker, who had signed my acceptance letter, was the Superintendent of Nurses. She was English. She had worked hard to establish strict, universally accepted standards for nurses' training, and to raise the level of recognition for nurses as professionals. Pennsylvania Hospital was ranked as one of the best in the country, thanks to her. I knew a lot would be expected of me here.

While taking courses, we nurses in training also worked in the hospital. My diary records many, many hours working on the wards and in the clinic. That did not leave much time to study. I was always very nervous that I would do poorly. Already, some of the Probationers had been asked to leave, or had decided they were not suited for this work.

As I was so much older than most of the other students, I had some trouble fitting into the routine. Unfortunately, I often arrived late to class or to my shift. Each time it happened, I would go on "report" and have to go to the Office. Each time, I expected to be sent home. On one trip to the Office, the Superintendent gave me an important piece of advice that I recorded in my diary: *"Life's movements are not forward, not upward, but straight ahead."* That made sense to me because that is how farmers approach life.

During the first quarter I was the lowest student in class standing. And yet, by some miracle, I kept progressing through each important milestone of our training. By the second quarter I had earned my way to number two in the class.

Anatomy and physiology; charting; surgery; tuberculosis; dissection; Materia Medica, fractures, infectious diseases and epidemiology, bandaging, massages, medicine…we had six classes a week, in addition to afternoon and evening shifts of duty in the hospital to give us practical experience in what we were learning. There were also lectures on the kind of conduct expected of us outside of class and work. After all, we represented Pennsylvania Hospital! We were strongly encouraged to donate part of our salary, once we began earning one, back to the hospital through a fund-raising system called "subscription".

> *"Sat. May 19, 1906: Miss Walker gave us a talk this morning at class. Advising the class to wear white shoes & stockings & also as to our conduct for the street & giving by subscription; laid emphasis on how to give."*

Because we provided our own uniforms, I sewed my own. My several uniforms took 42 yards of fabric – light blue, floor length, long sleeve dresses, with crisp white aprons and bibs. I look so proud in the official photograph taken early in my training.

Not only did we provide medical services to the patients, we also were responsible for their hygiene – giving tub baths or sponge baths as appropriate. I kept track of the number of "tubbies": thirteen one night, fifteen the next night, and on and on. The schedule was taking a toll on me. Several times I fell asleep in church on Sunday mornings.

The work was hard, but I made the most of my free time. Occasionally, I would get an afternoon off duty. My beloved aunt and uncle who lived in West Philadelphia, reachable by trolley. They always welcomed me, spoiling me with attention and good food. Sometimes, we students would get special permission to attend a concert in the city. There were other breaks in the routine as well.

> *"Sat. Nov. 17, 1906: We, the first section of the class entertained the 2nd section on the fourth floor, 8th St. home. All were dressed in ridiculous costumes. Front room was used as the dining room, having four small tables; decorated in blue and white. All had very nice time. Refreshments,*

ice-cream, chocolate eclairs, cocoa, small cakes. I bought a new hat last Wednesday at $3.75."

Nurses were not immune to illness, especially since we were always so exhausted and run down. It was hard on us when one of us got sick. Not only did it mean more work for the rest of us who covered the shift, but also, we tended to our fallen colleague so carefully. Usually, a special nurse was assigned to her. Sometimes there was heartbreak. It was my habit to record in my diary the name of every patient who died so she or he was memorialized forever. That was a custom I continued for the rest of my career.

"Sat. Jan 5, 1907: We had eight operations today & I will be busy all night."

"Tues. Jan 8, 1907: Miss Lively and Miss Kreutzen are very sick, delirious at night; Miss Haughton is specialling them."

"Sat. Jan 19, 1907: Miss Lively died this morning at 1 o'clock."

A scarlet fever epidemic broke out during my last semester in training. It was extremely contagious, especially dangerous for children, and was spread by person-to-person contact. The crowded conditions of city life were a perfect place for it to take hold. Many city children worked long hours in factories under terrible, unhealthy conditions. Schools and businesses closed because of the epidemic. Newspapers all over the country listed the number of new cases each day and described precautions for quarantining. Our hospital was full. Sometimes, we had to ship the sickest ones to the Municipal Hospital across town. We had few areas that could be used to set the scarlet fever patients apart from the rest of the building.

"Wed. Feb. 1, 1908: South ward was isolated yesterday afternoon by hanging a sheet over the door & always keeping it wet with carbolic acid solution. There are 9 children in there & the nurse caring for them cares for them alone. No one else except the Resident going in. Another child was taken away this afternoon. Miss Chishome cares for the children in the day time. Miss Smedis at night."

"Thur. Feb. 2, 1908: Jimmie Avello developed scarlet fever & was taken away this evening."

"Sat. Feb. 4, 1908: Morman Thomas was taken away this evening to the Municipal Hospital."

As our graduation drew near, I found myself quite discouraged about the work. We had 21 patients on the ward. The death of one of them affected me deeply. Her name was Sally Miller. She was a diabetic, who developed a gangrenous foot, just like Mother. Her suffering made me think back to Mother's last days, and the events that propelled me into nursing. I recorded it in my diary.

"Sat Mar. 22, 1908: I was impressed by the death of Sally Miller, a diabetic patient with gangrenous foot at 3:15 p.m. "

Our final days in school passed by quickly, with a flurry of activity.

"Fri. Mar. 10, 1908; We had examination in Electricity this evening."

"Sat. Mar. 22, 1908: My white uniform is finished for commencement."

"Fri. Mar. 27, 1908: We had an oral examination in Surgical technique by Miss Gordon in Miss Payne's presence at 1 p.m. The class did well. Each one was examined separately."

On May 26, 1908, twenty-three of us graduated from the Pennsylvania Hospital Training School for Nurses. The keynote speaker gave us a talk called "Be Prudent". A dozen of my relatives were my guests at the ceremony; Father did not attend.

"Wed. May 27, 1908: I went to the office at 7 o'clock this evening. Had a little talk with Miss Payne. She said I had done good work and had improved very much this last year. Also, that she would give me a position in her School when she had a vacancy if I would take it. She gave me my diploma and thirty-two dollars and ten cents in cash, what was left over from my text-books. I am about all packed, there is my trunk and a large

package that I shall express; then I will have my suitcase and a package just as large as the suitcase to carry with me. I never thought I had so much."

"Thurs May 28, 1908: I left the Hospital for home this morning at 8 o'clock, took the trolley and got to Burlington at 11 o'clock. Met Howard and drove out getting here for dinner. Had a strawberry short-cake, very good."

"Fri May 29, 1908: Emma and I met Aunt Annie at her home and drove to the Cedar Hill Cemetery this afternoon, to put flowers on the graves."

For the next two months, I returned to life on Father's farm. I helped pick strawberries for market, canned corn and other early vegetables, and attended annual picnics put on by all the local churches. It was a chance to catch up on old friendships. As always, I sewed and sewed and sewed. Then, another opportunity knocked.

I was accepted for a two-month graduate course at the Sloane Maternity Hospital in New York City! I would be living in the nurses' residence at 408 West 57th Street, attending lectures, and working with patients. It was to be an intense session.

Emma took me to the train in Burlington, and I headed north, arriving in New York at 6:00 p.m. I had a terrible time finding my way to my boarding place, although I asked three times. My room looked out on a lot of tenement houses and there were a number of children with their noise and that of the street. This was busier than Philadelphia, and certainly a far cry from the noises of the country! That first night I slept poorly.

Right away, I was assigned to the nursery – twenty-four babies! I trained in helping deliver the babies and assisting in the operating room. The work was demanding, and the hours were erratic. In my diary I recorded the number of births each day, and my schedule. Sometimes, I was out of sorts from being pushed and pulled in so many directions at once.

"Mon Sept. 21, 1909: I had a very hard night. First I went to the operating room, about 8:30 I went to the third floor, I was called back to operating room, took one case and went back to third at 10:00. At 12, I went

to second floor and at three I was sent to operating room again at 3 and
got back again to 2nd at 5:45 a.m. With all the work to do there and the
floor new to me, no one to help, nor even a waiting woman coming until
about 7. It was very hard. I had to go back. Mad!"

What wonderful things I discovered in the city during my few hours of free
time! I enjoyed walking through Central Park, especially the menagerie. It
was good, but not better than the zoo in Philadelphia. Whenever I could, I
attended worship services, going to a different church each time. Letters from
my family and friends were always welcome, and I answered every one. One
afternoon I wrote seven letters!

Finally, my training came to an end, and I was called into the Superintendent's office to receive my certificate of completion. Something else awaited
me there too: a job!

"Sun. Oct. 24, 1909: Miss Hutchinson called me in her room to talk business; and offered me the 4th floor in the near future as the supervisor of
that floor was to leave. I was much surprised."

Now, Emma and I both possessed something none of our foremothers ever
had: an income! A steady, regular, predictable income! Independence!

1909 – New York City

What a whirlwind! Within two months I had gotten used to my new work, and felt I was steadily improving. I was much older than many of the nurses; all of us were unmarried, and addressed each other as Miss ---, never by our first name. We all lived in the nurses' residence of the hospital and got to know each other very well.

There was so much to do in New York, and I took advantage of every free afternoon or evening. Little by little I found my way around the city by subway and elevated train. The Natural History Museum was one of my favorite places to visit. One day I walked across the Brooklyn Bridge. Often, I went swimming at the Y.W.C.A. early in the morning when it was almost empty. There were sound and light concerts in Central Park, excursions to Coney Island, and so much more.

As much as I enjoyed my job and living in that exciting city, it was always good to go back to the farm for a weekend. Train connections between New York City and Burlington were good. My brother Walter had returned from the sea, gotten married to Sarah, and had a farm of his own outside Columbus. I would send him a letter telling when to expect me, and he would pick me up at the station in our horse-drawn wagon. Sometimes, if there wasn't time for a letter, I would surprise Father by walking home from the train. Rob had come back to the farm to live, and the two of them were there alone. I noticed that Father's health was beginning to fail, and Rob was poorly also. They needed me. In February 1911, Sloane granted me a leave of absence to go home and nurse the two of them. Father and Rob passed away at the farm within months of each other. They joined Mary Ella, Mother, and so many more at beautiful Cedar Hill.

Father was the youngest of thirteen children, seven of whom died as infants. He was only nine years old when he lost his own father, so their household was tinged with sadness. Before he and Mother married, he had gone to Indiana for work that would help relieve his family's financial difficulties. Then, he spent many years trying to provide for all of us. One by one, we all abandoned him. Some people described Father as mean. Maybe he was just lonely.

My brothers settled the affairs at Father's farm. Someone else would live in the old home place now. Walter, Howard and John had their own farms by this time, Clif was in Detroit building automobiles for Mr. Henry Ford, and Oscar was working as a machinist in an amusement park in Ohio. He was also learning to fly an airplane. Walter bought a truck from one of our cousins, which made taking his produce to market so much faster.

Emma was teaching in Oil City, Pennsylvania, near the western border of the state. In our frequent letters to each other, we began discussing an idea. Magazines were promoting the joys of cross-country travel, which was becoming quite popular at that time. New roads and railroads made it possible to go places we had never dreamed of before. Both of us had a lot of experience using trains, so we got a copy of the Official Railway Guide, and began planning an adventure to take before I returned to my job at the Hospital. I would meet Emma in Oil City, we would stop to visit Oscar and Clif, and keep going until we reached the Pacific Ocean. I remember the table in my old diary that said it was 3,100 miles from Philadelphia to San Francisco. We were so busy I didn't even have time to write about it in my diary! It took us three months to complete the round trip. Only three years earlier San Francisco had been destroyed by a massive earthquake and fire. When we got there, the city was in the midst of an exciting state of recovery and rebuilding. It took root in

Emma's heart. I wonder if even then she was thinking about how she could return. As for me, within a few years, I would make an even more epic journey of my own.

It was time to return to Sloane. My old job, and a salary of $55 per month, were waiting for me. I received a warm welcome back. In my diary I noted that my feet minded the hard floor, and my ears minded the noise. I would have to get used to both again. I got back in time for the Women's Suffrage parade on Fifth Avenue. There were tens of thousands of women marchers of all ages, dressed in white, carrying banners that said things like "A vote for suffrage is a vote for justice!" It was quite a spectacle.

The mood of the city was changing. Europe and the Balkans had been in political turmoil for some time. I didn't understand the details of the conflict, but the newspapers were full of events and speculation. More and more countries began entering the fray. That summer, war broke out overseas. We called it the Great War because so many countries were involved, although it is known now as World War I. Terrible things were happening. After our American Civil War and the Spanish-American War, many people were tired of bloodshed, and insisted that our country remain neutral. But the truth is, we were already heavily involved.

One July night we were thrown from our beds by a huge explosion, followed by another, that rocked buildings and smashed windows. The whole sky lit up. A freight train carrying two million tons of munitions blew up on an island in New York Harbor. Fires broke out. Warehouses and piers were destroyed, barges and tugboats sank. It was rumored that thousands of people had been killed. By daylight, gawkers began flocking to the scene to try to collect souvenirs and view the damage. A friend and I took an excursion boat to visit the Statue of Liberty, hoping to see for ourselves. We were not allowed to land at the Statue, which had been scarred by the blasts, but were taken to Staten Island instead. We soon learned that it was an act of sabotage by German agents, trying to stop the supplies the United States was sending to help Great Britain and its allies defend themselves against the invading Axis nations.

The next spring, the United States entered the Great War, in support of Great Britain and its allies. For some time, the American Red Cross had been raising funds and recruiting personnel to provide medical and humanitarian aid to the regions caught up in conflict - Europe and Asia Minor. A gentleman who had spent eight months in the war gave an interesting lecture with lantern slides, explaining the hospital work he did overseas. With some of my fellow nurses, I attended the massive Red Cross parade in Brooklyn. It was stirring! First came bands and regiments of the New York State Guard, First Cavalry, and Naval Battalion units marching in review. They were followed by 10,000 women in Red Cross uniforms, thousands of children who were in the new Junior Red Cross, ambulances, and floats. That evening, I attended a huge rally at Carnegie Hall. I made an important decision: I wanted to join the Red Cross and do my part to help war victims abroad. I was moved by the stories of immense suffering, and on August 21, 1918, I submitted my application for service.

The United States troops sent into the war helped bring it to an end in November. New York City erupted!

> *"Thurs Nov. 7, 1918: the Express says Germany has surrendered this pm.& the whistles have blown all p.m. & the city is wild this evening. Everyone is out with horns & bells; the din is more like New Years"*

> *"Mon. Nov 11, 1918: Germany signed the Armistice & the city is in an uproar; Miss W & I went out this p.m. & evening. Streets crowded, good natured & noise began at 5 a.m."*

PART II

1919 – Near East Relief

The Armistice with Germany ended the Great War, but the need for humanitarian aid was more dire than ever. Hundreds of thousands of destitute refugees faced disease and starvation. The war had displaced thousands of people, left many orphans, destroyed means of earning a living, and changed national borders. Genocidal massacres had taken place in Armenia. Local hostilities continued. The centuries-old Ottoman Empire was crumbling under the attack of British forces, which by then were occupying the Turkish city of Constantinople, along with French and Italian troops. The Turks, in turn, were fighting to rid themselves of foreign occupiers and control adjoining lands. Greece was laying claim to that territory as well. British victory in the Russian Caucuses and unrest in the remainder of that country were forcing evacuation of masses of humans fleeing for their lives through Asia Minor.

I remember from pouring over the maps in my diaries that there is a thin peninsula connecting the part of Turkey that is in Eastern Europe to the larger part of the country which is in Asia. The peninsula provides a land bridge for refugees escaping Europe. The narrow Bosporus Strait, running from the Black Sea to the Sea of Marmara separates the European from the Asian continent. This area of the world was known as Asia Minor. The surrounding territory of Lebanon, Syria, Iraq, Palestine (now called Israel) and Jordan was referred to as the Near East.

The Red Cross had forwarded my application to the newly formed American Committee for Relief in the Near East, known as A. C. R. N. E., which accepted me for duty in Turkey. My appointment card and badge arrived on September 10. I was so pleased to have them! I was one of the American nurses on the way to help!

On Sunday, February 16, 1919, I boarded the transatlantic passenger ship Leviathan, docked in New York Harbor.

> *"Sun. Feb. 16, 1919 – The Leviathan left dock at 6:30 A.M. , most everyone went on deck to watch the embarkation. It seemed strange & dreary to be leaving on such a journey. We were at breakfast when passing the Statue of L., but watched the last of the land disappearing in the west."*

The only way to cross the ocean was by ship. Airplanes in those days, like the one my brother Oscar learned to fly, were only big enough for one or two people, and only flew short distances before needing to stop and take on more fuel.

The ship Leviathan had been used by the United States government to transport soldiers and supplies to Europe during the Great War. Later, it would be reconditioned into a luxury liner, and would be one of the most popular passenger liners of the time. But when we boarded, it was still a bare basic troop ship fresh from the war.

My previous shipboard experiences had been the Delaware River steamboat travelling between Burlington and Philadelphia, and the New York Harbor ferry. This ship was indeed a leviathan – a giant! Other Americans on the ship were headed to Turkey, like me. Some young men were volunteers for the new Y.M.C.A. set up in Constantinople. Others were teachers going to one of the two American colleges there. Fifty-four women were nurses in the same program as I. This was not like the sea cruises of today. We slept many to a room, in bunk beds or berths. There were no activities or entertainment provided for us on the ship. We arranged all our own. We held exciting competitions, like tug of war, to pass the time. It rained for much of the seven-day journey.

When we docked in the French military port of Brest, there were American soldiers waiting to board for the return home from the Great War. So many men! Immediately after we got off, fourteen thousand of them would board the Leviathan to head back across the Atlantic. Fourteen thousand passengers on one ship! The newspaper said that all were boarded within two hours because the process had become so efficient.

From Brest we were transported almost six hundred miles from one coast of France to the other on a hospital train furnished by the United States government. We were crowded, but comfortable. Because it was a special train, not on the regular schedule, we were often sidetracked to let other trains pass through. This was so different from my train travel at home.

The savage battles of the war had occurred north of where we were traveling, so we saw little of the ruin. Much of the winter landscape we passed through was covered with water, a great flood from melting snow or rain. Fields were small and quite cut up, compared to the farms in New Jersey. Gardens had stone walls around them, and the houses were stone also, with one end used as a stable. How different from the farms on which I had lived! We were only allowed one short chance to stretch our legs before getting back on the train. It took a long time to reach Marseille.

The next leg of our trip was aboard a British hospital transport ship across the Mediterranean. The sea was rough, and I was quite sick for the first days. As the weather improved, and the sea grew calmer, I was able to enjoy the journey. How thrilling to pass by Italy and Crete! On a balmy morning five days later we anchored in Salonica, an ancient city on the coast of northeastern Greece. This was the first city I saw with minarets. It was very hilly.

In Salonica we began to see evidence of much neglect and poverty, such as beggars in the street, a result of years of war. This was our first taste of the reality of what we were getting into. We acquired a new crew, and continued steaming toward our assignment.

Ah! Land! Temporarily, we were housed on the Greek island of Prinkipo while we got ourselves sorted out. The island was already being used to keep German prisoners of war, but they were to move out soon. Originally, these had been summer homes for the wealthy people of the city. We saw Armenians and Turks. As I walked around the island, I was struck by how different it was from anything I'd seen before.

"Wed. Mar. 12, 1919 - Many gardens with flowers. A few vegetable gardens. Donkeys & goats are the only domestic animals here. Some chickens. Streets have narrow sidewalks & everyone uses the middle of the road to walk in which are good mostly. Very few wagons of any sort. All carting is done on backs of men. The Armenians of Prinkipo gave us a reception on Tuesday evening. It was very nice."

"Thur. Mar. 13, 1919 – We rested and enjoyed a walk on the island."

Then our work began. We were transported to the outposts of Dirindje and Ismed located near the Turkish border, where we began unloading and organizing relief supplies to set up hospital stations for displaced persons and others in need throughout the region. We were surrounded by a barbed wire entanglement for about a mile in every direction, which extended right down to the water on the beach. The hills around the village were etched with dug-out trenches and dotted with white military tents, each with armed guards. The largest trench was for us to use in case of bombardment. There was still active combat in the region between Greek, English, and Turkish nationalist forces and remaining Ottoman holdouts.

Here, I began regular nursing duty. Windows of buildings were covered with sandbags. The wall of the cemetery had a large hole for the machine guns used to defend the post. So far, our patients were suffering from a variety of illnesses or from accidents. There were eight nurses. We systematized the work and were able to manage it in twelve-hour shifts. We got along well, and made quite a happy little family. We had relaxation, but no recreation, as there was nothing to do around there. So, we made picnics. In addition, we were often invited to dances and teas on board the American and British

Naval ships in the harbor of this major military area. These social outings were quite lovely.

> *"Thur. Mar. 20, 1919 – Cold, rainy, raw. I am assigned to look after the sick members of the party with three others. Dirindje is where all the relief supplies are stored, 2 big stone houses & three or more smaller ones. The equipment shipments are made up here & sent to the various Stations. Everyone is helping to categorize the supplies, also getting and equipment ready to go to the Caucuses."*

By early April, my group was ready to head to other posts. We boarded an American submarine chaser ship, then transferred to a train along with units destined for Smyrna, Konia and Ouchak. I made lots of notes in my diary.

> *"Tue. Apr. 8, 1919 – Fair. The Smyrna Unit goes tonight at 6 p.m. consisting of 20 cars & 15 more under leadership of Dr. Pratt. Konia group goes at same time & same train."*

> *"Fri. Apr. 11, 1919 – Clear, warm, calm. Arrived at Ouchak about 11 last night. It is a pretty place with farming land all around. Hills in the far distance. Also snow-capped hills. Grain at every station. Arrived here about 11 last night, natives tried to board our car. Mrs. Pratt called "Hidar" & they left & door was closed. This place seems like a junction, a large open station filled with grain for shipping, some cars loaded. Six good rough cast red tile roof, one story houses, trimmed in white, gray shutters. The station is two stories & family living above it or it is used as a hotel. A number of locust trees 6 to 8 inches in diameter. 2 to 3 doz. men sitting around. Mostly a goodly number children, women always out of sight. A few small white-wash buildings back of yards which seem well kept, a few red & white lilac bushes & roses. Men wear the Turkish fez."*

I was stationed in the beautiful ancient waterfront city of Smyrna. Even though I didn't write much about it, the situation here was tense. It was a city mostly of Turkish Muslims, with some Greeks and Armenians. The harbor was full of French, Italian, Greek, British, and American war ships. Greek forces were scheduled to begin a three-year occupation of the area as part of a peace treaty that was to be signed soon after our arrival. The Greek residents viewed the occupational army as liberators; the Turks viewed them as invaders. The landing of twenty thousand Greek troops in Smyrna for the signing of the peace treaty soon turned into a riot. Stores were looted, and hundreds of Greeks and Turks were killed. Our fledgling hospital was spared from the looting and we simply kept working, treating as many of the wounded as we could.

After that, things here calmed down as the Turks surrendered to the occupiers. There were only a few minor incidents of soldiers opening fire on the hospital. The hospital in Constantinople was not so fortunate. For days it was under siege as Turkish fought against French and British forces for control of the hospital building. Finally, as in Smyrna, the Turks surrendered, but there were many casualties there.

It seemed strange at first, but quickly I felt like I had never lived anywhere else. Greek, Russian and Turkish nurses and doctors joined our staff. We did not speak each-others' languages, but made do very well with gestures and pointing. The bigger difficulty was the difference in culture. Our director explained that there was no nursing tradition in this country to build on, and strange prejudices and attitudes prevailed toward the work. Women had no role in the professions. In addition, there was dislike, suspicion and misunderstanding among the various nationalities of nurses, staff and patients. I remember one of the first emergency patients I treated. In fact, I wrote home to my brother about it.

> "This & yesterday have been very hot & of course dry as we have had no rain since the latter part of May & will not again until the middle of Sept or first of Oct. Also this hot weather unlike that of U.S.A. will continue for the next two & a half or three months. We were told this is the usual weather for this season of the year except it should commence about the middle of May & no rain after the first. We are told this has been an unusual spring & summer so cool & we called it warm & at times almost hot, I see now by the two days just past what they mean by hot weather & it may be even hotter. None of the people here seem to mind it as we

do. They wear more clothing than we do I think. Don't use many buttons in their clothing, almost everything is tied on regardless of sex or age. An emergency case was brought in the other day. A man. The "tram" (horse car) ran over him crushing one leg half way below the knee & the toes on the foot. He was in a bad condition & naturally I helped to undress him. His coat was unbuttoned & removed in the usual way. Then I attempted to remove his trousers which were fastened & held up by a strip of calico yards long, perhaps an inch wide tightly fastened around his waist just below the band of trousers in an invisible way. Out came my scissors & that string was in two pieces as quick as the wink of an eye & the leg of trousers were ripped in a jiffy & another snip of scissors & off drop the outer garments. Then underdrawers came next, there were tied on even more securely & with much more & wider "string". When I finally saw his waist it was smaller than a "Lady of Fashion" in "84-86" or there abouts. The question of how the men keep their clothes on in this country is a sore one with the doctors, the yards of string that one man uses is surprising.

"Since coming to the hospital we did not get around much, do not have time & are not off together besides it is too hot to go out before about four or half past in the P.M. We live in the building in nice rooms but a bit crowded. There are a lot of unpleasant things we have to put up with & there are many pleasant ones to offset the former. The evenings are somewhat cooler than the days. If we lived higher on the hill or nearer the bay we would get a nice breeze. We have no trouble getting on the right side of our patients even if we don't speak their language. We get along fine with signs. Some of the nurses can talk just beautiful with their hands & head, yes surely the whole body assists. I find myself following their example."

The "Lady of Fashion" referred to in the letter was something that always made my brother and me laugh. As a child in the 1880s, when my cousin and I poured over fashion magazines, the stylish ladies shown in them had tiny waists that were cinched in with stiff corsets. Of course, this made it difficult to breathe, and caused damage to internal organs over time. In extreme cases, some women even had their bottom a rib removed to make it possible to for tighten the corsets even more. Even though I loved the pictures, I never tried to copy the trend for a tiny waist.

Letters from home took months to arrive. News from home made me realize the differences between rural New Jersey and where I lived now. I still wrote as many letters as I always had, trying to think of things my family and friends would want to know. Emma was still teaching, but wanting a change. The boys were all raising young families. Whenever possible, I sent my letters along with Naval officers, college professors, Y.M.C.A. volunteers and others who would be returning home. My brother John teased me about getting a letter written Smyrna, Greece, with a United States postage stamp, posted from Philadelphia. When I left New York in January, John and his wife were expecting their second child. It was almost Christmas by the time of learned of my new little niece.

We never tired of watching the people of the Near East. Greeks, Turks, Jews and Armenians all had their particular style of dress and customs. Having enjoyed swimming so much at the Y.W.C.A. in New York City, I soon discovered the delights of the Greek sea front. I did not take a bathing costume with me, so I had to acquire some wool flannel and sew one for myself. I am sure the Greeks, Turks, Jews and Armenians got as much amusement watching me in my bathing costume as I got from observing them.

Most of my life had been spent on a farm, so I was always interested in what produce we found in the markets. There was so much variety! Some of it I recognized, others I did not. Much of it was what I considered to be of poor quality. However, I realized that the orchards and gardens had been untended for years because of war.

> "The loads of tomatoes I see coming into market are tied to donkey's backs, two big baskets holding about a bushel & a half & one fastened on each side of a donkeys back, there may be one such donkey or any number up to fifteen or more two there is the usual number. Occasionally there is a cart load which may hold eight-or ten-bushel baskets. Their carts are really two-wheel wagons for when the donkey is hitched, they are level like a wagon & have springs under the body. One of our young doctors calls them

"bone shakers" for this cart or wagon is as often used to take the whole family & that of the neighbors for a "carriage ride" & all sitting on the floor even to the driver & if it is too full the feet may hang over the edge."

In October, I was allowed a week-long leave of absence, which I chose to spend in Athens. I never would have believed that I would really be in Athens if it were not for the fact that so many unbelievable things had happened to me already in this past year. My guide book called Athens "a real European city", but I had not seen a European city before, so I wouldn't know if that was true. While there were lots of modern stores, everything was very expensive. In my opinion, Smyrna's bazaar could easily beat that of Athens, which was small, though interesting.

"We saw uniforms & uniforms about the city; they were mostly Greek & I wondered how one army could have so many kinds. There were black uniforms with brass buttons, brown uniforms with red pipings a soft red skull cap & a handsome 2-inch black silk tassel hanging from the top over the left shoulder. There were uniforms with bright red trousers, others blue trousers & bright red stripe down the outer sides; there was ash-gray & khaki & dear knows now many others. The officers or many of them looked real 'nifty'.

"Then there was the peasants' dress which to me was equally as interesting & more curious, & I believe beyond my description. There is one which I call a perfect <u>wonder</u> worn by the men, consisting of white stockinet leggings or tights reaching from the ankle to hips from shoes turned up toes & a three inch (in diameter) black pompom on them. A white skirt (looked like cambric) reaching almost to the knees, <u>very</u> full. I was told that one of those skirts measured forty yards in width & I could easy believe it for just ruffles & ruffles & ruffles. With sleeves reaching to wrist, a sort of ebon jacket of blue cloth trimmed with black braid & a girdle. A soft red felt skull cap with a black tassel completes the custom. And whenever I look at this specimen I was thankful I did not have to see to his laundry. Some of the women wore very full skirts & long & always with an apron. Aprons are very fashionable for girls women & small boys up to 10 or 12 years

"We went to & from Athens by the Greek Red Cross hospital boat. Before the war it was the king's yacht. This boat trip was as enjoyable as Athens itself. To see the Gulf of Smyrna from the boat was so different from the view one gets from land. And the sea was so blue, a different blue from the Atlantic, almost a royal blue, looked just as if the sea had been dyed."

Later, I had another new adventure – a Turkish bath. A group of us went to an old, ornate marble building with separate entrances for men and women. I wore the flannel bathing costume I had made, but other wore much less! We were in a hot, dry room, which created quite a sweat. Then, a woman attendant scrubbed us with a refreshing lather. I was told that it promoted good health and relaxation. This was a treat I'd like to have again.

"Tues. Dec 9, 1919: Had my first Turkish bath. Some experience!"

"Sat. Dec. 19, 1919: Cloudy. Sewed all day. Went of a home visit to see triplets 3 days old. Weigh 3 ½ to 4 pounds each. Very strong."

1920 – The Hospital

Constantinople! At last! After months of setting up outpost hospitals, I finally reached what was supposed to be my destination. The table in the front of my diary says the distance between New York and Constantinople is 5,810 miles. Another table says the Turkish piaster is worth four cents in American money on the gold standard. We reached there the evening of January 1. It had been snowing. Except for the minarets, the landscape looked like it could have been western Pennsylvania. There were fifty-four nurses in our unit. We were to establish an eighty-bed American hospital, educational center and nursing school. The goal of the school was to train our own replacements, provide medical care for the English-speaking residents of the region, and create new employment opportunities for the local women as nurses and other staff.

We were escorted to number 13 Rue Petits-Champs, the building that would house our new facility, and could not believe our eyes. It was the harem of the former pasha's palace! Completely unsuited for a hospital! The three-story building was in poor repair, large rooms had windows on only one side, there were rough wood floors, and no heat or plumbing of any kind. The water supply was uncertain. We immediately nicknamed our quarters "Paradise".

The facility was antiquated and inadequate, with few conveniences. I wrote letters by a lamp so poor it was no better than a candle. My room had an old-fashioned oil burner that did not work. I spent all my spare time over four days getting it to burn. That did me little good; there was such a scarcity of fuel in this country, that we were always cold. There was no laundry room except for an outside cistern and scrubbing board that had been for a single family. The marble Turkish toilets were very different from what we were used to, and there were few of them. Our work was so laborious because of the primitive conditions. A major victory was the completion of a steam system that delivered hot water to the laundry and kitchen!

There were so many orphans, so many children in need of clothes, food and shelter! Much of my free time was spent sewing for them, using donated fabric. We handed out warm winter clothing at the clinic and sent it to the A.C.R.N.E.-run orphanages, which were usually in empty school buildings. Due to the war, schools had been shut for years. We called the one in Alexandropol "Orphan City" because it was the largest orphanage in history. People were doing the best they could for these children, but conditions were terrible. Any illness spread rapidly, especially among malnourished children. At one point, there was an epidemic of Tracoma – pinkeye- which caused great discomfort. Besides health issues and lack of clothing and other supplies, feeding so many orphans was a challenge. Our reports showed that A.C.R.N.E. was feeding more than ninety thousand children, either in orphanages or at soup kitchens throughout the Near East.

Newspapers all over the United States carried the story of the creation of the American Hospital in Constantinople. It said our hospital was to eventually become the nucleus of an important American medical center in the Near East. And, there was my name! Right there in the paper! "Miss A. Estella Sutton" was to be one of the nurses. The article said that the need for a hospital for English-speaking patients was urgent because American firms were opening branches in Constantinople every week. Already, there were two American colleges run by the Methodist church, one for men and one for women, as well as a branch of the Y.M.C.A. The American businesses were moving in to open new markets and occupy the vacuum left by the chaos of war. Both the Y.M.C.A. and the two colleges saw the opportunity to spread Christianity in a part of the world dominated by the Muslim and Orthodox religions.

After the initial work of getting the American Hospital set up, I found the job to be boring and disappointing. I was working shifts on the hospital floor and running the clinics for outpatient medical visits. It seemed so unimportant. The hospital was established to care for Americans and the British living in the city. None of our patients were combatants or victims of the turmoil going on around us. This is not why I joined the Red Cross. In New York I was touched by the sad humanitarian plight in this part of the world, as it had been presented to me, and wanted to help. My work in the outposts had been fulfilling, but this was not.

At first, all our patients were men. It was many months before we got our first woman patient. That was probably to be expected because our English-speaking population consisted of American teachers and businessmen, British diplomats and their wives, and military men. Our biggest excitement was an emergency appendectomy on a British sailor.

The clinics were not busy, cases were mild. The Greek, Turkish and Armenian student nurses being trained in the school were required to work in the hospital and clinic to gain practical experience along with their studies, just as I had in my own nurses' training. They were indifferent to their tasks and unsuitable for the work. Many were dismissed soon after they were admitted. Looking back on it, I realized that the young women students saw themselves as caring for the foreign occupiers instead of for their own people who needed them most. Suddenly, another door opened. There was revolution in Russia!

Hoards of Russians were evacuating Kiev and Odessa, which had fallen to the Bolshevik revolutionaries. By February 1920 there were ships filled with over 150,000 men, women and children in the harbor. It was said they were packed so tightly onto the ships that it was impossible for them to lie down and they had to take turns at it. It was cold. There was insufficient food and water. They were not allowed to land while the powers in charge of the city determined what to do with them. Constantinople was already exhausted and overburdened with displaced people and orphans, and in no condition to take on additional responsibilities. After more than forty days in the harbor, the ships were redirected to a Greek island – Proti. I was temporarily reassigned there to take care of the Russians.

There were sixteen of us assigned to Proti. We arrived in three feet of snow, with neither equipment nor supplies other than blankets. Immediately, we began getting three abandoned buildings ready to receive the Russians. On February 10, in a blinding blizzard and fighting rough seas, the ship Navajo delivered the first eight hundred refugees to our island. We brought ashore those who could walk. The next morning, after the storm had abated, we carried in the sick, the wounded, and those too weak to walk.

> "Wed. Feb. 11, 1920 – Proti. Clear. Not too cold. Been working all day getting three houses ready to receive the sick Russian refugees. Supplies have not come & we have only blankets."

> "Thurs. Feb. 12, 1920 – Clear. The island like a fairy land – beautiful. Began to unload the refugees last evening about 8 p.m. & we worked until 1:30 this a.m. I have hospital 2 & it is full but crowded in more today. Now there are 55 up & down stairs so thick on the floor cannot walk without stepping on them."

One of our first tasks was bathing our patients and delousing them. Most of them had typhus, a disease caused by filth, transmitted by lice. They had escaped their homeland with nothing but the clothes on their back. They had not bathed nor had clean clothes since they fled. They were destitute. They were in shock, exhausted, disoriented, grieving, starving and traumatized. I wrote about what followed in a letter to my brother:

> "It was two weeks ago yesterday on the 10th of Feb. that four Red Cross workers & several A.C.R.N.E. workers & about four Y.W.C.A. workers were gathered together by the American relief & sent to Proti about five miles by boat from Constan. to be ready to receive help to care for a boat load of Russian refugees that were due here then but landed here the day after because of the storm. There were about 16 of us & we worked until 1:30 a.m. that night getting them housed & fed. About 250 were wounded & sick. Many of them had to lay on deck in the open the boat was so

crowded. They came from Odessa driven out by the Bolsheviks. Many were lousy & all were dirty, some had money & others were penniless. All were a sad sight. Many froze their feet or hands so that the nails came off & they have as bad looking toes & fingers as you would want to see. But all are on the mend now, that is the surgical cases. There is much typhus here several new cases yesterday, but I did not hear of any this a.m. but there are many new cases developing daily. We have had five deaths. We are in for an epidemic & I hope we are equal to it. I think we are as we have the people half cleaned & the clothing nearly all deloused.

"We are very, very busy as the Russians do not understand our ways & we do not understand theirs so there is no team work going on although a few are beginning to fall in line."

We had opened up three hospitals in less than a day: one for contagious diseases; one for surgical work; and one for medical work. Five hundred abled-bodied persons walked up the slippery, stony, practically perpendicular incline to the monastery, which was the only available building on the island big enough to house that many. There, we opened a kitchen, bathrooms, delousing stations, and store rooms. The Y.M.C.A. established a passport office to help sort out where these people might go when their quarantine was lifted. The once silent monastery with its quiet gardens had become a busy village. By mid-February, there were over a thousand refugees on the island.

Our A.C.R.N.E. newsletter called the Acorne reported on one of the happier incidents of that first day. "*The first day stretchers arrived at the hospital faster than beds could be prepared, and distracted orderlies and nurses were rushing about trying to make room for more patients. The surgical hospital was packed when another stretcher was brought up the steep path, and deposited at the foot of the steps. "But we can't take any more," said the agitated nurse. "Who is it?" "Je suis un femme," said a quavering voice. The nurse rushed down and lifted the blanket. "Good heavens! It's a baby! A day-old baby!" And it was: a tiny, scowling, wrinkled morsel of humanity asleep in its mother's arms, totally oblivious to the distressed doctors and nurses. The concerns of that Russian mite, swept in by the Black Sea on a storm-tossed, typus-infested ship was ludicrous.*

For the first time everyone laughed. Needless to say, the baby found a home – a good one – on the island of Proti."

Like the young mother, many refugees spoke French. That language was spoken by highly educated Russians, and those who had been part of high society. These elite comprised a large number of the people fleeing the populist Marxist Bolshevik revolution.

Eventually, Russian doctors and nurses who had also fled their native land took over the medical part of hospital work. My colleagues and I tended to running the houses. It pleased me to see many of my earlier patients begin to recover. Some of them performed Russian dances and songs for us. We were even able to explore and enjoy the island.

With the Russians now taking care of their own, it was time to go back to the city. My temporary reassignment ended, and the whole Proti staff went to the dock to see me off. I wished I could be two people; one would stay in Proti. To me, the work there had so much greater value, and was so much more interesting than the hospital work I had been doing in Constantinople.

Before reporting to duty back at the American Hospital, I was given time off to recuperate. I knew just what I wanted to do with it: Egypt and the Holy Land! By the middle of March, I was on my way!

> *"Mon. Mar 15 , 1920– Constantinople. Fair. Off for Egypt. Hurrah. Our party is Misses MacIntosh. Janson, Coughlin, Mrs. Stevenson, Mr. Duerr & I. And we all feel very sure we will have a nice trip. How wonderful to be on my way to Egypt."*

> *"Tues. Mar. 16, 1920– Fair. At 1 p.m. 214 miles from Constant. A delightful voyage. I can hardly believe even now that I am on my way to Egypt. I am so happy to be realizing what to me seemed an impossible dream."*

Oh! What a trip! I visited Bethlehem by carriage…saw Jerusalem on a cloudy day…ate lunch in Jericho… washed my hands in the Jordan River, which was muddy and swift… bathed in the Dead Sea… attended Palm Sunday services at the Church of the Holy Sepulcher…went to Bethany and saw Lazarus' tomb and the house where his sisters Mary and Martha lived... traveled by donkey to the pyramids... continued on to Alexandria. In Cairo we had to wait several days for passport and visa paperwork. Since we had to stay until the red tape was completed, I was asked to help out at the hospital there, and found that I liked it very much. Very quickly I learned my way around the city, and felt comfortable there. When it was time to go, I boarded a ship taking sick Turkish prisoners to Constantinople. I was sorry to leave Egypt.

Unexpectedly, I was sent back to Proti for the purpose of closing part of the compound down, and opening a tuberculosis unit in a nearby monastery. My daily chores ranged from burning trash, which I hated, to making curtains for the offices of the new facility, since we as yet had no tuberculosis patients. My director and several of the important Russians and people in the relief effort came to Proti to inaugurate the new hospital and spend July 4th with us. We had a lovely day.

Trouble continued all over the region. One by one, the outpost units from the interior of Asia Minor were closing because it had gotten too dangerous. Those nurses who were sent back to Constantinople had been through a hard time and were rather the worse for wear. Several had lost everything to raiders, and had barely escaped with their lives. The American compound in Marash was overrun; many were killed or wounded. That reign of terror lasted for days until the survivors could escape with the French Army. Even then, more died as they retreated through a blizzard along mountain paths. Aleppo, Urfas, Mardin...no word. Communications had been cut off.

We received notice of the evacuation of our A.C.R.N.E. orphanage in Adana. The children and staff were taken out under cover of darkness, on foot, stumbling over rocks and through streams. What a job keeping the frightened children hushed so they would not be discovered. Each carried a little cloth bag around his or her neck with the few belongings they could salvage. When morning dawned, the ragged band was fired upon by the Turks. This, thankfully, was ended by a retort from French cannons. We were so relieved when all two hundred in the party made it to the train station and safely came to Constantinople.

I was dividing my time between Proti and Constantinople. It was an eight-hundred-mile commute by boat across the Aegean Sea. Then, another crisis! The Proti hospital burned to the ground. It caught fire when ashes emptied from the pipe by one of the Russian colonels fell down a crack in the wall. All my beautiful curtains were gone! There was absolutely no chance to save the building. Fortunately, no lives were lost.

By July, severe fighting was just about three miles outside Constantinople, despite the treaties that had been signed. Renegade troops of the former pasha continued guerilla attacks in attempt to oust the foreign occupiers. Every day we would see some sort of horror within the city limits. Due to the influx of American businesses seeking new opportunities, one newspaper described our city as combining "all the frenzy of a new mining camp and a seaport". Despite that, the papers pessimistically predicted that it was "the end of the trail for all Balkan states everywhere"; there were no civil courts and no one keeping order. I wrote to my brother that conditions in this part had not improved, and perhaps had gotten worse. I told him we were safe and not one bit worried, that those in power were taking the necessary precautions to keep the violence from reaching us. Privately, I could not be certain this was true. With so many nations sharing post-war power, and others trying to retain it or regain it, there was rampant corruption and confusion. Rumors even flew that the Bolsheviks' ultimate goal was the taking of Constantinople.

To keep my mind busy, I began planning my return trip to the United States, making it the dream trip of a lifetime. I wanted to spend time in Italy and Paris. Once again, I was studying the maps in my diaries.

Actually, I was more nervous about returning to the United States than I was about staying in Asia Minor! Our local English language newspapers were reporting on labor unrest, dissatisfied veterans, unemployment, and inflation at home in this period following the Great War. And, what about me? How would I fit in now that I had lived these experiences? Who could understand what I had been through? I was so tanned and white-haired by now. My wardrobe was a mess. Because of my "advanced age", there was great discussion among my brothers about which one of them this spinster sister would spend the rest of her days living with. I would have to make a new place for myself, for I was not as old as some in my family seemed to think. I was forty-six years old.

"*Fri Oct. 29 1920 – I am getting so tired of the work here – will be glad when my time is up.*"

There were only weeks to go until the end of my contract, and my return to the U.S. I had started to pack my trunks. Suddenly, more Russians! The Crimea fell to the Bolsheviks, and eighty thousand refugees were crammed into ships headed our way. My supervisor asked me to stay to help with the onslaught. As there was no outbound passage available at any price, I had little choice but to remain.

In my diary, I confessed to being cross. Only a few Russians were admitted to our American hospital; they were not very sick, but very demanding. There had been some changes, which were causing tension among the staff. I was irritable because of the long hours and poor management. For example, I sewed uniforms for all the student nurses. My supervisor did not realize the work necessary to outfit one nurse – not to mention ALL of them - and constantly urged me to hurry. I got no time off, with sewing and looking after the laundry. I was sick of the whole place. Several of my dearest friends had already left. I wondered if I would be able to hold out until I was released.

"*Thurs. Nov. 25, 1920: Thanksgiving Day and I am not thankful. I know I am on the dark side.*"

"*Fri. Dec. 24, 1920: Christmas tomorrow. No holiday spirit here as we Americans are having it alone, the superintendent decided it so, all are opposed to her discussion but no help. So we lose all pleasure & we give gifts half-heartedly.*"

I was so tired and defeated.

Epilogue

In January 1921 Essie did finally leave the Near East. For more than a month, she enjoyed the sights of Italy and Paris, just as she had dreamed. One of her souvenirs was a packet of picture postcards she bought in Reims, showing the historic French city reduced to rubble by bombs and cannons in the Great War.

She returned home to a very much changed nation. When she left for the Near East, women had not yet gained suffrage. Once she got back, Essie registered as a Republican and voted for the first time. In 1918 few families owned automobiles. Thanks to innovations in automobile production, such as in the factory where brother Clif worked in Detroit, cars became more affordable, and there were many more on the roads. Radio broadcasting was becoming popular, as well as the new motion picture industry.

As for Constantinople, two years after Essie left, a government was formed by the revolutionary group led by Mustafa Kemal and his colleagues. They laid the foundation of the republic of modern Turkey. Kemal was given the title "Ataturk", or "Father of Turkey" by a grateful nation, and is still honored today. A decade later, the name of the city was changed to Istanbul.

Back in the United States, Essie nursed her sister-in-law, Clif's wife, through a terminal illness in Detroit. After that, she began looking for a warmer climate, and settled in Phoenix, Arizona. Arizona had only become a state a few years before, and was still quite vast and sparsely populated. There, she did private duty nursing, or "specials", at the local hospitals and also for wounded veterans in their own homes. The latter was paid for by the War Department, as there were no Veterans' Administration Medical Centers in those days. In Phoenix, Essie had a telephone in her home for the first time.

Eventually Essie moved back to Philadelphia, where she had gone to nursing school. With so much experience, she knew she would easily find employment there. However, when she began looking for work, she was told that she was too old to be hired as a nurse! She was only 51 years old! That did not stop her. She began visiting department stores, and got a job as a clerk at the Woolworth's 5 & 10. She loved the job and Woolworth's loved her. Even when many younger employees were let go after the busy holiday season, Essie was kept on board.

Another lucky opportunity presented itself. Her beloved sister Emma moved to San Francisco, where the two of them had visited so many years before, and bought a bakery. No one knows how or why. Essie went too; her sales and bookkeeping skills lent themselves nicely to helping out with the business. The Little Cake Shop at 2437 Fillmore Street was a success.

Although neither Essie nor Emma had children of her own, they were favorite aunts to their ten nieces and nephews. Essie would send them letters and packages with interesting tidbits she had picked up, such as a seashell, a dried flower, a pretty ribbon, a porcupine quill, a wooden chair carved from a broom handle, or an inspirational saying clipped from the newspaper. Each prize was wrapped in tissue paper with a note in her tiny handwriting documenting where she had found it. She spent little time with her brothers, but remained close through correspondence and short visits.

Upon her death after a long and interesting life Essie was buried in the Cedar Hill Cemetery beside her parents and little sister. There, she is surrounded by generations of her large extended family.

Essie's and Emma's resilience is inspiring. Their lifetime was a period of tremendous change. They were born in the horse-and-buggy Victorian era, and lived to see trans-Atlantic passenger air travel, automobile-choked highways, and telephones in almost every home. They saw eleven stars added to the American flag as eleven new states were admitted to the union.

Time and time again they reinvented themselves, and took control of their own lives. Their willingness to take risks and try new things served them well as they adapted to new situations, developing skills and self-confidence. In the process, they traveled, met interesting people, and left a lasting mark on those who knew them. They were legendary to family members too young to have met them, but who grew up being entertained with stories of Essie's and Emma's adventures.

In Gratitude

This is a special thank you to Lyn Wargny, who read every word of my first draft. Her careful proofreading, comments and questions helped me make this book more interesting and readable. I am grateful for the time she devoted to this project and for her expertise.

Margaret Marks is my life-long friend, who has helped me with countless projects. I value her keen observation, intelligent feedback, and unwavering support.

There are others who preserved and promoted the stories of Essie and Emma. My grandmother Eleanor Sutton thought her sister-in-law Essie's letters, diaries and trinkets were worth saving. That is how a large trunk of them survived. My mother Betty Robbins raised me with intriguing Aunt Essie stories. She read every single diary, which had writing so small, it required a magnifying glass to see. On each, she left notes that were useful in organizing the material many years later. Both Eleanor and Betty would be amazed and delighted by the publication of this book. Essie and Emma would be puzzled that anyone thought their story to be of interest.

Glossary

Affidavit – a written statement, done voluntarily and under oath, that is used to verify, make clear, or prove a set of facts.

Amputate – cut off, remove

Anarchist – a person who is against established order, such as that of a government

Asia Minor – the region consisting of what eventually became the country of Turkey The surrounding territory of Lebanon, Syria, Iraq, Palestine (now, Israel) and Jordan. The Black Sea on one side and the Sea of Marmara on the other side are its two coasts.

Balkans – also known as the Balkan Peninsula, this region today is Bulgaria. It is bordered by the Adriatic Sea, the Ionian Sea, the Aegean Sea ,the Turkish Straits, and the Black Sea .

Bolshevik – a radical, far left Marxist group led by Vladimir Lenin that created a revolution in Russia in 1917 and overthrew the existing government.

Catechism – a list of principles of a Christian religion, in the form of questions and answers, used for teaching. Children were required to recite the list from memory in order to move up into the next level of Sunday school.

Caucuses – the region spanning Europe and Asia, between the Black Sea and the Caspian Sea and mainly occupied by Armenia, Azerbaijan, Georgia, and parts of Southern Russia.

Christian Endeavor – "CE" was an organization for Christian youth that was popular among Protestant churches, beginning in the late 1800s. This was a chance for young people to socialize and learn leadership skills.

Constantinople - the capital city of the Roman/Byzantine, Latin, and Ottoman Empires. It was renamed Istanbul in 1930. Today it is the Republic of Turkey's largest city.

Crimea – the peninsula along the northern coast of the Black Sea. For centuries it had been part of Russia. With the Bolshevik Revolution in 1917, residents who had been loyal to the previous government were persecuted and fled for their lives.

Delousing – getting rid of disease-causing parasitic insects called lice by repeatedly laundering clothing and bathing infested people with harsh soap

Destitute – poor, deprived, suffering

Gangrene – a serious infection that stops blood flow and causes the death of soft tissues in the body. Left untreated, it is fatal.

Genocide/Genocidal - the deliberate killing of a large number of people from a particular nation or ethnic group with the goal of destroying that nation or group.

Gold Standard – the monetary system in which a unit of currency can be exchanged for its value in gold

Great War – now known as World War I (WWI) this was a global war that originated in Europe in July 1914 and lasted until November 1918. The United States entered the war in April 1917. It was one of the deadliest conflicts in history with more than 40 million civilian and military casualties and countless millions of displaced persons. It was thought to be "the war that ends all wars."

Guerilla attacks – combat in which small groups who are not part of a regular military conduct unconventional surprise ambushes, raids, or sabotage on larger traditional military units.

Harem – a separate, secluded place in a Muslim household where the women of the family, including female servants, live.

Lantern Slides – images are printed or painted on a piece of glass, through which a bright light projects the image onto a screen so it can be seen by an audience.

Leviathan – a legendary large, powerful sea monster

Long Depression – a period of world-wide financial depression which began in 1873 and lasted more than 20 years

Manure – animal poop, often collected from cow barns and horse stables, then spread on fields as organic fertilizer

Marxist – the political ideals of Karl Marx and Friedrich Engels, which later formed the basis of Communism.

Massacre – the brutal and deliberate murder of a large number of people at once

Minaret – a tall tower, often built as part of a mosque, with a balcony from which the Muslim call to prayer is issued

Near East - now more commonly called the Middle East. It is generally applied to the countries of southwestern Asia between the Mediterranean and India.

Ottomans – residents of the Ottoman Empire, a Muslim state that covered most of Southeastern Europe, Western Asia, and Northern Africa between the 14th and early 20th centuries.

Pasha – the honorary title of any number of wealthy, high-ranking officials in the Ottoman Empire.

Peterson's Magazine – a monthly fashion magazine published in Philadelphia from 1849-1892.

Physiology – the study of normal functions of organisms and bodily organs

Quarantine – a period of isolation after a person's or group's exposure to an infectious disease. It is for the purpose of limited the spread of the disease.

Renegade – a person who rejects or rebels against a group, religion, cause, or organization and behaves differently from others in that group, often by his or her own rules

San Francisco earthquake – On April 18, 1906 the northern coast of California was hit with a huge earthquake. The quake and resulting fires that lasted for days destroyed 80% of the city of San Francisco, California. More than 3,000 people died. It is remembered as the deadliest earthquake in United States history.

Scarlet fever – a bacterial infection commonly affecting children. Left untreated, it can lead to serious complications.

Scrapple – the smallest scraps of pork or other meat, mixed with corn meal and spices, shaped into a loaf. It is sliced and fried. Scrapple is a regional dish in southern New Jersey and Philadelphia.

Spectacles - eyeglasses

Spinster – an unmarried woman, older than the typical age at which a woman marries.

Suffrage – the right to vote in political elections

Sunday School – also called Church School, these are classes affiliated with individual churches, held on Sundays for the purpose of religious instruction of children and adults.

Tuberculosis – a contagious bacterial infection that commonly affects the lungs or other organs.

Typhus – a group of infectious diseases caused by bacteria which spread to humans through the bites of fleas, lice and chiggers.

Woolworth's - The F.W. Woolworth Co. was the first store that sold discounted general merchandise at a fixed price, usually five or ten cents, undercutting the prices of other local merchants. Woolworth's Five and Ten, as the stores popularly became known, was one of the first American retailers to put merchandise out for the shopping public to handle and select without the assistance of a sales clerk. (Source: *Wikipedia)*

Wrapper – light-weight bathrobe worn to protect one's clothing while doing chores, or to cover a nightgown, pajamas, or underwear

Y.M.C.A. – the Young Men's Christian Association, begun in the 1800s as a safe haven of Bible study and prayer, where young men could escape from the dangers of life on the streets. It became a world-wide organization.

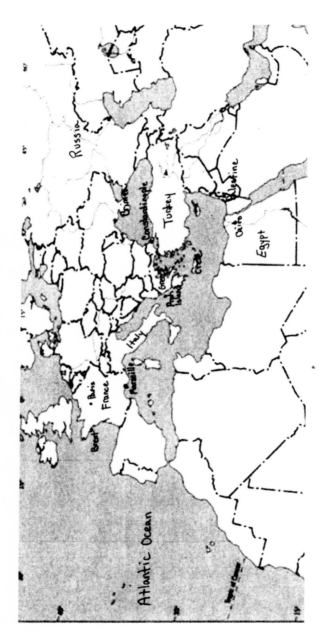

Miss Sutton's Journey to the Near East 1919-1921

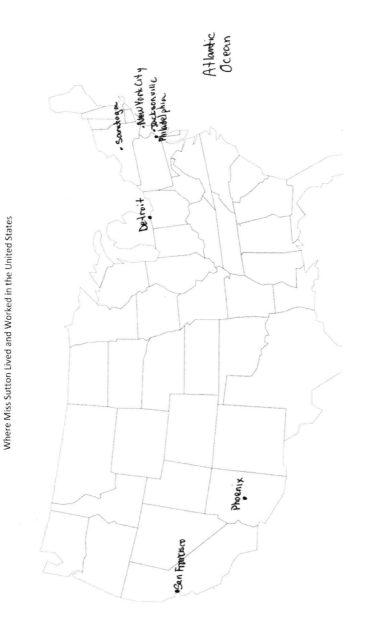

Where Miss Sutton Lived and Worked in the United States